Blush

Blush
Copyright © 2023 by Shefali Dang.

All rights reserved. This book or any portion thereof may not be reproduced or used in any manner whatsoever without the express written permission of the author except for the use of brief quotations in the context of reviews.

ISBN: 978-1-7380660

Book design & layout by Rachel Clift.
Cover design by Rachel Clift.
rcliftpoetry.com

First printing edition, 2023.

Shefali Dang
@theshefalidang

Blush

poems

SHEFALI DANG

for anoushka, laksh, and saahil

if you see my words drifting your way,

reach out for them and let them stay.

they have travelled so much, and travelled so far.

they carry songs of life,

the dark and light,

and all the things they have seen in between.

i pray they bring you a little warmth and some comfort

like they brought me on my foggiest days.

i hope you keep them close to your heart,

and when you do release them,

allow them to take a little bit of you with them —

just a tiny part.

TABLE OF CONTENTS

B – *beauty*........................ 1

L – *love*........................ 57

U – *understanding us* 107

S – *seasons* 137

H – *hurting and healing*........... 169

beauty

every poem i write is a love letter to you.

walk with me on my journey
and i will walk with you on yours.

let us talk about our deepest feelings
and biggest fears.

let us sit and count our scars —
i will show you mine
if you will show me yours.

let us explore the galaxies
in each other's eyes
and drown deep in the oceans
we call our souls.

let us forget time exists —

because time was never ours.

BLUSH

i wish you here on this dusty rose evening.
the day has settled and the night is yet to come.

the wind is flirting with the ocean waves
that want to be touched yet remain out of reach.

there is a salty recklessness in the air today
that is calling out to me,
that is serenading me with your name.

i wish you were here on this dusty rose evening.

when the wind whispers songs, long forgotten
memories wake up from their deep slumber —
the delicate fragrance of yesterday stirring up the soul.

it is a sweet walk down the path
we once called home.

there is so much movement in the day
and stillness in the night.
that is why, when the sun is out of sight,
secrets start spilling out
like fireflies, softly illuminating
the dark with their light.

let us go back to a time
when our smiles blushed
and our kisses were stolen.

when our eyes made love
and moments were frozen.

when our hands embraced
and feelings were conveyed.

when the world was ours
and we were so unafraid.

BLUSH

to be so delicate and yet so strong.

to shatter and still remain intact.

to be bursting with love and still feel light.

to be still and yet be the essence of life.

to feel so much and carry it all.

what a miracle the heart is.

these words that i have
will never be enough
to tell you how beautiful you are —

to tell you how beautiful you make me.

BLUSH

there is so much grace
in staying soft.

there is so much beauty
in being kind.

there is so much tenderness
in showing love.

there is so much soul
in being real.

if you could see

what i see,

you would fall in love with yourself.

she is a dreamer,
a deep thinker.

she is a mystery,
a secret keeper.

she loves too much,
she says too little.

she feels too much,
she expects too little.

she is a believer,
a lover, a healer.

she is a keeper.

BLUSH

there is so much i want to say,
so many thoughts running through my mind,
but every word i wish to express
screams the same thing:
judge a little less.
be a lot more kind.

the same heart that cries those crimson tears
and aches because it is feeling blue,
carries a universe of flowers within it —
little buds bursting with love,
just waiting to bloom.

the weight of this world seems weightless,
worries light as feather.
everything fades into oblivion —
yesterday, today, tomorrow,
when love mixes in the air
that surrounds us.

all we need are soft whispers,
telling us we are doing ok.
to drown out all this toxic noise,
to mix some colour in all this grey.

our minds are full of thoughts,
so many spectrums of feelings and words.
so why do we not pick the ones
that have the kindest hues?

the weight of the air that we breathe
is sometimes light, sometimes heavy,
for it has a life of its own.

it carries stories since centuries,
some told some untold.

it drifts in and out of dreams,
some fulfilled some unfulfilled.

it sees promises being made,
some kept some unkept.

it hears love songs written in hearts,
some sung some unsung.

it reads poetry, recited by the soul,
some shared some unshared.

it sees tears being shed,
some happy some sad.

it sees life,
some coming some going.

the weight of the air that we breathe
is sometimes light, sometimes heavy,
for it has a life of its own.

she lived with a heart too big ♡ in a world too small.

she found herself within herself —
a light in the dark,
the loveliness of her heart,
and the sweetness of her soul
stood the test of time.

all she had to do
was look beyond the pain
and see the resilience
behind the scars.

and you still choose to smile
when your heart breaks in two.

don't you know
your strength
is the most
beautiful thing about you?

tell me what makes your eyes
light up brighter than
all the stars in the sky.

tell me what makes you smile
so beautifully
like a flower stretching
into full bloom.

tell me where do you go
when you sleep peacefully at night.

tell me about your dreams —
do they smell like perfume?

tell me about the lanes
you fly over
when you dream.

tell me about the memories
that still make you weep.

tell me about the love
that your heart
writes love letters to.

tell me where do your eyes
disappear to
when you sip your coffee.

tell me about that world
because I want to see it
through your eyes.

tell me about
those sweet moments
that make your heart
burst with love.

tell me what makes you feel safe.

tell me, who do you belong to?

tell me how secure do you feel

in a warm embrace,

and how loved do you feel

seeing your lover's loving face.

tell me which melody

makes your soul sing.

tell me stories which your soul

keeps hidden.

tell me how from a poet,
did you become poetry too?

tell me everything
because I am here
to listen to you.

BLUSH

sometimes i wish i wasn't a poet,
but somebody's muse instead.
to have words of yearning
written lovingly in my name,
to be immortalized
on the pages of notebooks,
and to be the reason
in the quiet of the night
a poet picks up his pen.

i see you lost in thoughts,
your heart wishing for beautiful things —
sweet sunsets and warm sunrises,
a cozy love and everything a fulfilled life brings.

*a hug is the language
of the soul —
it needs no translation.*

vintage hearts
speak in flowers.
vintage souls
speak in poems.

BLUSH

she is a flower,
holding herself together
by her roots,
using every drop
of rain or tears
to make herself stronger.

when she is ready,
she will turn
towards the love shining on her
and open her petals
to reveal the
magnificent beauty
that she is.

we share easily
what we have in abundance —
love or hate,
kindness or anger,
soul or darkness.

BLUSH

when someone is kind to you,
accept it.
absorb it.
soak your soul in it,
and then share it with the world.

the best gift you can give someone is their smile

*meet me at
the edge of the world*

where dreams become reality.

BLUSH

there is so much softness
in a love that doesn't need words
to express itself.

it is ok to surrender yourself
and sit in silence sometimes.

it is ok to take a step back
and let life guide you
without putting up a fight.

BLUSH

                      silent prayers
drifting across the night sky,
softening the darkness
one word of faith at a time.

sand melting away under my feet
into the turquoise blue sea.

wind playing with my hair,
doing and undoing my curls.

sunshine caressing my cheeks,
making me blush a soft pink.

in this fleeting moment
i took in everything:
love, life, joy, and grief,
and made peace with it all
because i was one with nature.

i was one with me.

BLUSH

she was awkward and quiet
until her face lit up,
mesmerizing everyone in the room.

she was strange and fascinating,
like a flower at night
in full bloom.

i wish flowers could speak.
they would make wonderful poets,
narrating stories of love and heartache,
of blooming and withering.

they would talk about how
nervous fingers touched one another
when a flower was given
in the name of affection
and accepted in sweet surrender.

of how they played an important part
in the declaration of love,
in the undoing of hearts.

they would smile at the memory
of how their fragrance
reminded someone of their lover.

how they were tucked
safely inside a book
so that they could keep
those delicate memories alive forever.

BLUSH

the silver moonlight
calls to the shore,
teasing it to come
and read what it wrote.

it writes stories with its glittering ink
that flows with the water below.

stories of lovers
who loved too much
and promised a lifetime
only to drift apart,
because time wasn't on their side,
like the sea drifts away from the shore.

i wonder, *where do thoughts go?*

do they flow with the sand below my feet
rushing to elope with the turquoise sea?

do they sit on the petals of flowers
blooming and resting for a little bit?

do they fly to different lands
on the feathers of birds?

do they freeze in the cold
and seek shade in the heat?

do they fall in the rain
cocooned in little droplets?

do they slide down colourful paths
in the playground of clouds and rainbows?

do they linger on like a memory,
or do they drift with the wind that is already carrying
thoughts with it since centuries?

i wonder, where do thoughts go?

BLUSH

glitter on her lips,
sparkle in her eyes,
her heart was made of rainbows
and her soul was dipped in sunshine.

i am of the sky,
the moon, and the stars.
the place where dreams reside.
if you want to look for me,
do not look too far.

i am alive
in all the corners of your heart.

BLUSH

i love the moon.
so stark against the dark,
like she knows her worth
and is not afraid to be seen.

the best conversations happen over coffee

BLUSH

soul to soul.

when things start falling in place,
it will not always happen
with a boom or a bang.
it could happen as softly as a whisper
or as delicately as a landing feather.

a house full of love.
a room full of books.
a kitchen full of food and laughter.
a passport full of stamps.
a heart full of peace.
a soul full of poetry.
a life full of experiences.
a legacy full of stories.

That is how I want my life to be.

we are
heartbeats and breaths,
moments and memories.

we are
the magic between
dreams and reality.

BLUSH

i was living a meaningless life,
forgotten and forgettable
like an untold piece of poetry,
collecting dust on the last page of a notebook
which never saw light
until you came along
and put back the rhyme in my song.

now i'm a love song,
sitting on your lips,
hummed from dusk to dawn.

i remember you —
the way you would catch my eye
and hold it prisoner for an eternity or two.

your deep voice, sinking into my soul,
like gravity belonged to you.

i remember us,
so drunk in love,
untouched by reality.

oh, how i wish i didn't, but
i remember you.

BLUSH

you brought me a rose
everyday that we met.

you told me you loved the way my hair smelled —
it was your favourite perfume.

you said my honey coloured eyes
changed the way you looked at this world.

it cleared up your vision, yet left you mesmerized.

i waited everyday for you to call me after work
and say you are coming to see me.

i loved the conversations over coffee
that turned into dinner,
that turned into long drives.

all the time in this world seemed too little for us,
but yet we never gave it a name.

you knew and i knew.

we knew.

it was too special to call it ordinary,
and here we are, years later,
smiling at the memories we created
because now we know
what we have is vintage love.

what we have is gold.

late into the night,
a few bottles of wine,
boundaries loosening with time,
racing hearts
stumbling over heartbeats,
so many tangled feelings
rushing forward while still frozen in time —

just two people falling in love
like poetry and rhyme.

BLUSH

drunk on love,
intoxicated on you.

if i could sing,
i would serenade you with a love song.
but a singer, i am not.
just a person
with some ink and a poet's heart.
so i declare my love on paper —

a love song in a love letter

you have a way
of finding your way
into my poems,
the shape of my words
have started looking a lot like
you.

you were the missing piece.

you were the   piece.

BLUSH

roadside cafes
and lipstick stained coffee cups.

dreamy eyes
and smiling lips.

lingering glances
setting the butterflies free.

hand in hand,
strolling the cobbled streets
under the blushing sky.

soft kisses
surrounded by fluttering hearts.

whispers of love,

you and i.

there aren't enough
i love yous
in this universe
to tell you
how much
i love you.

BLUSH

if i were a story,
would you read me over and over again?

if i were a song,
would you wrap me in your breath and hum me from dusk to dawn?

if i were a memory,
would you visit me once in a while?

if i were the moon,
would you look up at me with a smile?

if i were a moment,
would you freeze time?

all those messy feelings,
ruffled hair and crumpled bedsheets,
lazy smiles and red wine —
i was yours
and you were mine.

BLUSH

so beautiful was our first kiss,
that before fading into the night,
even the sky blushed a pretty pink.

if i could steal time,
i would —
for the stolen moments.
for the stolen glances.
for the stolen smiles.
for the stolen kisses.

forehead kisses

are kisses meant for the soul.

there are love letters in my heart
that i write to you everyday.

love letters i don't send
with words i never say.

BLUSH

a little drunk,
a little tipsy.
a little wine,
a little whiskey.
a little you,
a little me,
and
a little bit of eternity.

when he gently brushes your hair aside,
when he quietly wipes the tear that escaped your eye,
when he falls apart to keep you together,
you know he is the one.

the one who will keep you safe
and never leave you alone in the dark.

the one you can never let go of
because he is the one who has your heart.

BLUSH

i love how
i'm falling in love with myself
as i'm falling in love with you.

you are my favourite moment.

when life broke me
and i broke you because of life,
you were still my silent strength.

— thank you

BLUSH

i know sometimes it is tiring,
trying to keep the boat afloat.
trying to keep things moving smoothly.
trying to straighten
every crease and every curve.
sometimes it is so hard to hold on,
and tempting to give up
and free ourselves from this roller coaster.
sometimes it is easy to ignore
the grip that we have
that is so tight,
it is still holding on and not letting go.
sometimes it is easy to forget
that we are still here
only because
we really want it much more
than we don't.

frozen in time,
stuck in a place
where the heart longs to be,
replaying memories
of a time long gone by,
where your voice still echoes
in sync with my heartbeat.
where your fragrance
still lingers in the air,
and your kisses
whisper sweet nothings onto my skin,
like poetry written
for just you and for me.

there are a million
love letters
silently floating around
in the silver moonlight,
in the golden of the day,
in the lazy breeze of the oceans,
in the desert sand, twirling away.
in the sky, sliding down rainbows,
in the fragrance of roses,
in the sweetness of honey,
in the misty streets,
in the half sunny horizon.

and in the softness of the morning dew,
there are a million love letters
finding their way
from me to you.

there is something so
beautifully endearing
about writing a love letter.
you strip your soul bare
and pour all the love
brimming in your heart
onto paper,
your pen trying to keep up
with the flow of your thoughts
while your heart runs wildly,
tripping and stumbling
up and down your stomach
in nervousness and excitement.

there is something so innocent
about reading a love letter.
you hold the letter in your hands
while the blood rushes to your face
and paints your cheeks a pinkish red.
you gently undo the soft folds
of the paper
while your soul comes undone
and drowns in the words
floating before your eyes.
you read it over and over
until you memorize
every curve of every letter.
until you can measure
the depth of the ink,
making the words on the paper
a love letter.

BLUSH

i am till this heart beats,
and this heart beats
just for you —
i am just for you.

let us slip into something more comfortable, like each other's soul.

i don't know how you do it.
i'm the one with the words,
but you still leave me speechless.

it is the tenderness
in the moments
that make them eternal.

even the folds of the love letters you once wrote to me
are holding on to the words inside ever so tightly.

BLUSH

i blew kisses softly into my words,
knowing they will reach you someday.
and when they do find you,
i hope you will let them stay.

for me, the shape of love
is not a heart,
but a circle.
a small circle, but a strong circle,
full of love and warmth.

BLUSH

every flower
pressed within the pages
of an old book
has a story to tell —
a story so beautiful and delicate
that it still carries the fragrance
of those love affairs.

i keep coming back to you,
and you keep coming back to me.
tell me this isn't gravity between us.
tell me we aren't meant to be.

sometimes melodies get attached to memories.

i feel like my heart has swallowed
roses and peonies.
it's glowing with pretty hues.
or maybe that's just what
being in love does to you.

BLUSH

lying in the aftermath of passion,
the scent of destruction lingering in the air.
we belonged to one another, in that moment.
in the same way,
a sunset belongs to the sea.

so beautiful but so temporary.

being in a healthy relationship should feel like
coming home at the end of the day,
stripping down to your soul,
and settling in to the comfort of your bed.

BLUSH

why am i here, you ask?
for you.
for us.
for the things
we will never know we could be
if we don't take this chance.

your name echoes from deep within my soul
from eons gone by —
soothing, calming, and unconditional.
a constant
in the ever changing days.
a place for me to undress myself
until i'm all flaws and bones,
knowing here, i am safe
like never before.
your name
wrapping me like a lullaby.
blanketing me in it's warmth,
floating weightlessly in my heart
until i feel myself unfold.
your name —
one that has stood the test of time.
something which only i know.

— friend

and just like that,
the darkness collapsed
to let the light through.

all it took was for me to
finally look at myself
and say,
i love you.

allow your heart
to break into an applause
and cheer for you
every now and then.

BLUSH

some days you just want
someone to tell you
how amazing you are,
and some days
you need that someone
to be *you*.

my skin is glowing,
my smile is wider,
my eyes are twinkling,
and my soul has never been happier.

i love what
being in love with myself
is doing to me.

i'm watching myself bloom.

BLUSH

gift yourself some roses.
pour yourself some wine.
look at yourself in the mirror
and fall in love with that beautiful smile.

you know you do your best
to keep everyone happy,
and somedays it takes all of you
to stop dimming your shine.
let go of your worries
for just a little while.
make right now all about you.
right now is your time.

understanding us

BLUSH

waterfall and mountains,
the river rushing to meet the sea.
you sat there by the banks,
waiting to say those three words to me.
i didn't know that would be the day.
i didn't see it coming.
i wish i had known
so I could stop it from happening,
because somethings are best left unsaid,
and some dreams are best left unseen.
but that day,
the cool breeze and curious waves
got to witness the beginning of a nightmare
and the end of a dream.

we were never meant to be.

we were a potent dose of heaven and hell.
a reckless affair of softness and sharp edges.
we were an intoxicating cocktail of truth and lies —
a tragedy dressed as love.
we were everything we shouldn't have been
and everything that wasn't meant to be.

look at what I've done.
you kept me in the dark,
so I made you my sun.
i was lighting up our world,
but you burned us down
even before we had begun.

you are here
but you are
not there.

BLUSH

you mattered more than you'll know.
you mattered more than i'll say.
but what mattered was,
when things got tough,
you were the first to run away.

i gave away all of me for so little of you.

BLUSH

drunk enough to remember
everything i had thought
i had forgotten about you.

tell me,
how many times did you try to forget me
before you realized you could not?

tell me,
how many sleepless nights did you have to endure,
only to fall asleep and dream of me?

BLUSH

you still exist
in fragments of my imagination —
a kaleidoscope of memories
floating in brightly coloured hues.

my heart is heavy
with the weight of you.
it is pulling me down.
it is making me slow.
all this holding on
is making my soul hurt.
i am opening my palms
and letting you go.

trapped in the past,
i had caged my heart,
holding my breath in hope
until i could no more.
my legs, unable to move.
i was drowning
because I had forgotten
how to float.

i peeled you off
like dead skin i didn't need.
and now that you are gone,
i am, finally, able to breathe

BLUSH

don't hate me for letting you go.
i just couldn't hold on anymore.
i tried so hard to be what you needed,
but all this pressure was driving me crazy.
i loved you so much,
but i wasn't being faithful to me.

i was tearing myself down
so you could rebuild me the way you liked,
from the way i talked
to the way i smiled,
but that's not how it works.
we knew it was never going to last.

you wanted everything your way
from the moment we started.
it's my fault i kept quiet —
i didn't want things to fall apart.
i tried to make you happy,
but no matter what i did,
it was never enough.

i was never enough.

tell me,
how many songs did you listen to
just to get over me,
only to have that one song drift towards you
when you least expected?

that one song, which was mine.

a day might come
when we will breathe the same air,
so close,
but souls apart.

don't come looking for me,
because the girl you once loved
won't be there.

buckling under the weight of it all,
the years of being strong
and the years of breaking down.
trudging through non-stop,
we came undone.

— fractured love

how can i imprison you with my love
when your love has set me free?

i hope when you remember me
you think of pink roses.
a soft reminder of the love we once shared.
of the things we knew but left unsaid.

where do we go from here?
what do we do?
everything seems so dark and blurry.
even the heart and mind are confused.
there are decisions to make
and steps to take.

the crossroads of life
are calling out to you.

we were a messy love story —
not perfect in any way.
intense and tender,
passionate and soft,
letting go, holding on.
all that could go wrong, did.
but in the end,
what mattered was,

we stayed.

BLUSH

we crashed.
we burned.
we disintegrated into dust.

all that remained was
the madness,
the stubbornness,
the desire to remain together.

and so,
fighting for every puff of breath,
blowing life back into us,

we rose like smoke.

i drank in our moments,
soaked myself to the bone.
little did i realize,
i was growing roots there,
and making you my home.

BLUSH

like a feeling
that lingers,
like a fragrance
that stays in the mind,
like a fleeting moment
that becomes eternal in the memory,
like a kiss
that forever stays on the lips,
we are forever
through space and time.

we are two parts
of one whole.
two hearts and one soul.
like salt and pepper,
like ink and paper,
like frost and heat,
like pain that is bitter and sweet.
like a journey and its destination,
like a high rise grounded by its foundation,
i flow like a river.
you guide me like my shore.
i fly freely like a kite,
yet your love holds me close.
we are two parts
of one whole —
both different.
both equal
neither is less, neither is more.

BLUSH

perhaps i was holding on too tight.
perhaps you were not holding on at all.

perhaps i was too involved.
perhaps you felt indifference would not harm us.

perhaps i was looking for perfection.
perhaps you knew nothing is ever perfect.

perhaps i should have loosened my grip a bit.
perhaps you should have held on a bit more.

perhaps there was never really an us.
perhaps there was just a you and me.

perhaps you and me had to fall apart to come back together as *Us*.
perhaps we were always meant to be.

perhaps the timing was all wrong.
perhaps now is when we were meant to meet.

perhaps we had to break to put the pieces back together differently.
perhaps a new balance was what was needed.

perhaps that was the beauty of all this.
perhaps this was destiny.

the weight of the unspoken words
hangs cautiously between us,
like a dense
yet delicate fog.

we don't speak,
for we fear what might happen
once the trance is broken
and the words are spoken.

*holding on to these
little moments
of us holding on to one another.*

your soul is as deep as the sea,
as vast as the ocean,
and i've only just begun
to drown.

seasons

BLUSH

it is that time of the year again
when everything turns to gold,
like a sweet sunset,
whispering goodbye,
only to wake up with a newness again.

it is that time of the year again
when summer melts in the arms of fall.
when the crisp air falls in love
with the sun kissed leaves
and steals them from its trees.

it is that time of the year again
when change is in the air
and the soul just wants to be free —

when letting go is the only way
to start over again.

everything is changing —
the air is cooler,
the leaves are redder,
the skies are darker,
and the nights are longer.
everything is changing.
summer has kissed goodbye,

just like you and i.

BLUSH

blurred lines fading.
memories evading.
the heart still tries to hold on,
but like autumn,
everything is changing.

we fell like shedding leaves,
spiraling down,
spinning helplessly,
unable to hold on to what once was.
we crashed onto the ground.
from blooming flowers,
we became beautiful debris.

BLUSH

she shed her tears
under the autumn tree.
the falling tears
became one with
the fallen leaves.

it is beautiful to watch
the sun kissed leaves
break away from it's trees
and dance freely
in the tipsy autumn breeze.

BLUSH

fallen petals are beautiful too,
for they have grown,
endured, and learned to let go.
they carry whispers of life
as they softly fall away,
and free the stories they have seen,
letting them become one
with the nomadic air.

when the golden of the day
fades into the silver of the night,
when the summer falls into a wintry slumber
and springs back to life,
will you still be there?

when the skies
crack open and unburden their soul,
when the flowers stretch in full bloom
and then slowly wither,
will you still be there?

when our thoughts get tired
and the words stop pouring out,
when the journey is closer to the end
and we sit down, content that it even happened at all,
will you still be there?

BLUSH

in the scorching heat,
when you feel a sudden
chill in the breeze,
know that is me,
right next to you.
when the falling leaves
fall on you and refuse to leave,
no matter how much you brush them away,
know that is my love,
showering down on you.
when even on the coldest day,
you feel a warm flush in your cheeks,
know my hands are touching your face
because your face is all i see everywhere i go.
when the rain pours down
and the flowers start to bloom,
know i miss you
with every single breath and beat.

can you hear the love songs blowing with the autumn wind?

BLUSH

i wait for you
like the darkness waits for the light.
i wait to feel your breath
because your every breath is mine.
i wait for the sun to rise and set.
i wait for the seasons to change.
just come back to me
because it is time.

our love was like different seasons —
you were already at fall,
while i kept waiting for you at spring.

and if you must fall, then fall like the autumn leaves —
beautifully and gracefully.

you must know
you are the warmth on frigid days,
the light illuminating the dark skies.
you are a galaxy within itself,
not just a star drifting by.

BLUSH

the air is less frigid.
the sun is out longer.
there is a softness all around
now that spring is around the corner.

there are days when i'm in a daze,
a figment of my own imagination
half here, half there,
neither drunk nor sober,
like spring in october.

BLUSH

i watch
the storm clouds rolling in
with thunder announcing its arrival.
the sky bursting open
and unburdening its grief
in front of the world.

i'm praying for the clouds to part
and the sun to come shining through.
i'm waiting for the light
to scare the darkness away.
i want to come home to myself —
i just need to find the way.

BLUSH

i fall for you
like the falling rain,
so helplessly,
yet so willing.
so fast,
yet frozen in time.

how will we grow
if we aren't willing to
stand in the rain
and get soaked
to the bone?

BLUSH

i'm listening to the music of life —
the swishing of the waves,
the rustling of the leaves,
the wind chimes dancing freely
in the warm summer breeze.
rain tap dancing on my window,
flowers blooming languidly,
stars snuggled in the arms of the night
and waking up to birds chirping sunnily.
zooming cars,
bustling cities,
excited chatter,
of people talking about their dreams.
the soothing voices of parents.
the stories of the wise elderly.
curious little minds
making sense of this world in their own innocent ways.
the tinkle of laugher.
the flutter of lashes.
cheeks turning an intoxicating red
at the sweet shy glances.
the intensity in the air
making the souls sizzle and melt into one another
while cupid's feathers tickle the butterflies in the stomach.
oh, how melodious is sound of falling in love.

i'm listening to the music of life —
the way life pulsates to its own beat.
the way this world breathes.
so won't you come listen to this music with me?

i've lived many lives in this lifetime so short.
i've lived for eternities in moments so few.
i've grown, bloomed, withered, and bloomed once again.
for i have lived the through the cycle of life
many times between sunrise and sunset.

BLUSH

would we wait for the sunrise
if it wasn't for the dark nights?

would we look up and admire rainbows
if it wasn't for the stormy skies?

would we stop to smell the blooming flowers
if it wasn't for the cold winter time?

would we appreciate kindness
if we hadn't been through some tough times?

would we value love more
if our hearts hadn't at some point broken and cried?

there was music playing in the background.
the waves were dancing joyously.
the salty breeze kept pushing my hair aside,
humming songs it has sung since centuries —
the melodies rich in memories,
the memories rich in stories.
what a beautiful evening it was,
when i sat quietly by the sea,
letting nature be one with me.

nothing brings more peace
than the sound of the ocean
crashing into your soul.

when was the last time
you sat under the sky
and counted all the stars?

when was the last time
you became one with
the sound of the open seas?

when was the last time
you let yourself flow
like the desert sand, aimlessly?

when was the last time
you let the breeze
caress your hair and kiss your cheek?

when was the last time
you looked up at the clouds
and looked for shapes in them?

when was the last time
you closed your eyes and stretched your arms wide,
and let the rain soak you completely?

BLUSH

let yourself feel
whatever it is you are feeling.
let yourself *breathe* in
whatever the changing seasons bring.
let yourself *heal*
one stitch at a time.
let yourself *grow*
one breath at a time.

don't belong to me,
for i don't belong to you.

i belong to the sun at noon
and the late night moon.

i belong to the desert sand,
which will always slip away from your hand.

i belong to the ocean, vast and deep,
and the mountain that is too steep.

i belong to the late evening mist
and the rose the morning dew kissed.

i belong to every breath that i breathe
and to the soil underneath.

i belong to your heartbeat
and the pain of love that is bitter and sweet.

i belong to this universe,
like a sacred holy verse.

don't belong to me,
for I don't belong to you.

hurting & healing

BLUSH

she has a messy heart
full of feelings
that sometimes hold her together —
other times rip her apart.

deep down, we all know
we deserve so much more,
but we still settle for less
because we fear the unknown
that comes after the letting go.

*do you even see me
when you look at me?*

we met when we were young.
you swept me off my feet.
i was so in love, and you said I was your dream.
when you said we were forever,
i thought you meant it.

and here i was, thinking we'd grow old together,
but you were out of the door before i could even blink.
little did i know
there are many ways to define forever.
i thought you would always be mine,
but for you, i was just a moment in time.

all our dreams of us doing things —
christmas shopping to evening strolls in spring,
sitting by the beach on sunny days,
to sharing a blanket by the fireplace —
were never really a part of your future, were they?

so blissfully happy, so sure i had it all,
never questioned anything, never even had a doubt.
i was living in a fool's paradise,
maybe even a little colour blind,
because i couldn't see all the red flags in sight.

and here i was, thinking we'd grow old together,
but you were out of the door before i could even blink.
little did i know
there are many ways to define forever.
i thought you would always be mine,
but for you, i was just a moment in time.

BLUSH

i lost myself to you
when i found you.
now that you aren't here,
i don't know
who to look for —

Me or You?

that's the thing about memories —
there're here to stay,
be it in a song
or the things you used to say.
i've tried locking them up,
hiding them from myself
in distant corners of my mind,
hoping someday they will simply fade away,
but here's the thing —

they sneak out of the darkness
and creep up on you when you least expect it,
like the perfume you used to wear,
lingering softly in the air.
the sky, just the right concoction
of a sultry white and blue.
like the day you said, *i love you.*

what am i to do with all these memories
that are leaving me heavy and empty at the same time,
filling me up with sadness and taking my breath away?
what am i to do with these memories
when you aren't here,
and i chose not to stay?
memories that i wish would go away,
but they follow me,
day and night,
night and day….

i wish memories
were unfaithful too,
but they stayed,
unlike you.

there is a strange sense of freedom in letting it all go.

you once told me i was like the open sea —
vast, breezy, and free.
i was colours you had never seen,
and words you had yet to read.
an ocean of newness,
something of which you had only dreamed.
you said i was someone out of your reach,
right there, but not really.

little did i know you were telling the truth.
i was the freedom you sought —
a little whiff of fresh air
in your life, so dull and grey.
a little saturation
in your monochromatic hues.
a craving you didn't want to curb.
an obsession you succumbed to.

and now, with your appetite satiated,
you disappeared into the sunset,
looking for new prey.
another day, another feast,
and i'm still here.
i'm still an open sea,
crashing into myself,
drowning into the vastness that was once me.

BLUSH

it is unsettling how some people
come close to you
because of your warmth,
then they light up a match
and watch you burn
until your soul is in ashes,
and all that remains
are little embers, fading into dust.

then they tell you,
it was your fault all along.

perhaps it is our boundaries that set us free
and walls that let us breathe.

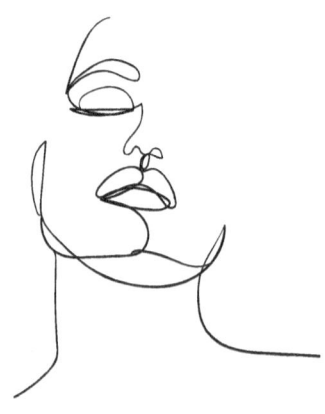

have you ever tried talking to loneliness?
it talks.
it isn't as silent as one might think.
it is full of stories,
and questions that remain unanswered,
and melodies that you thought
you had forgotten to sing.

i wish i could tell you how hard life has been.
i wish i could tell you i smile for the world while
i am crumbling within.
i wish i could collect all my tears and trade them for a few smiles.
i wish i could smooth out the lines that pain has dug into my skin.
i wish i could show you how tough every step forward has been.
i wish you could see the chains tied to my heels.
i wish you knew how i struggle everyday to not fall back
into the arms of my bed and sink into it for the rest of the day.
i wish my eyes were bigger so you
would have seen the sadness residing in them.
i wish my voice was louder so you
would have heard me when i told you i was feeling lost.
i wish i never let go of myself,
because now the path to myself is dark and unlit.
i wish the fog would clear and my search
for myself comes to an end.
i wish you had just held me and told me just once
that you were on my side.
i wish i knew it would be like this.
i wish i could just sleep for a little while and wake up
to a different time.

i collapsed under the weight of it all,
crashing into myself,
drowning deep into my shell.
i couldn't carry on anymore.
it was getting so hard to be me,
so i let it happen.
the sinking.
the breaking.
the crumbling.
the undoing.
thinking this was the end.
little did i know
i was growing,
and this unbearable pain
was just from me breaking free from myself.
i was growing, and i needed more space to stretch and bloom.
my old shell just wasn't enough anymore.
my world was evolving.
my soul was expanding.
and my heart did what it does best —

it kept on beating,
teaching me to love myself once again.

— growing pains

*as the heart grows stronger,
it also becomes lighter.*

BLUSH

the mountains that once seemed too steep to climb
now look like mere pebbles.
the gallons of tears i've shed everyday and every night
now seem vital in the cleansing of my sight.
every heartache was just that —
an ache, a pain
of growing into myself.
all those times i felt my world had collapsed
was just me shedding another layer.
i understand it now.

i was just getting ready for this beautiful life.

i'm unravelling myself
and facing my demons.
i'm coming undone,
unfurling and unfolding.
it's messy and terrifying,
but I'm ready to spread my wings.

BLUSH

she had shaky hands
but a steady stride,
a nervous heart,
fainting in fright.
her soul was determined,
and faith, unwavering,
so she took the unfamiliar path
and walked towards her dreams.

for she wanted to meet herself
when she was on the other side.

there will be those
who will come into your life,
suck the light out of you,
and leave you in the darkness.

then there will be those who
will make you shine so bright
by just being there.

— choose wisely

*poetry hugs people
when they need it the most.*

i found your memories
in a chest of things i didn't want to see.
they were lying there, in a corner,
abandoned, lonely, and insignificant —
just the way you made me feel.

clinging to the fibres of my dress,
the hem coming apart at the seam
from the weight of it all.
maybe i collected them on my way out,
that dress too, i never want to see.

i packed you away with all your promises,
the lies, and deceit,
in the darkness of the chest
because darkness is all you could give me.

i promised myself i wouldn't turn back.
i promised i would never visit the past.
but here i am, holding my breath,
with the chest open in front of me.

amongst things long forgotten,
amongst things i just didn't want to see,
you resemble dust now —
so i blow you away and set myself free.

BLUSH

i drank so many cups of coffee,
sitting, lost in thoughts of you.
thinking i was found.
but i was a fool and had no clue.
i didn't know then, that darkness doesn't come announced,
nor does it come with thunder and gloom.
it can walk into your life with arms open wide,
flashing a bright smile,
and before you know it, you are doomed.

now i know better.
i might even call myself a warrior.
i cried. i screamed. i gasped for air.
then i dug my way out from there.

i grew, bloomed, and grew.

and now that i am where i wanted to be,
i can finally sip my coffee and enjoy the view.

i'm still trying to get to know myself
(the person i became after you).

BLUSH

somedays i feel you
out of the blue.
a sudden pang,
a skipped heartbeat,
a flood of emotions.
memories of you playing on repeat.
a broken heart, still trying to heal
from all the lies and deceit.

the soul doesn't understand rules of society.
it understands feelings and vibrations.
it is attracted to what makes it feel good,
and drifts away from what doesn't.

caught in a battle of wills
between my mind and myself.
although we're one,
we are not the same.
my mind paces back and forth frantically
while I seek to be still.

if you have to judge me,
judge me when my soul is at peace
and mind at rest —
not when chaos has handcuffed me
and put itself in the driver's seat.

when my eyes are smiling
and twinkling in joy —
not when they are sunken in defeat
and the light is barely there.

if you have to judge me,
judge me when i've made it through the darkness
and i'm basking in the sunlight —
not when i'm sinking in quicksand,
unable to see the right from wrong.

if you have to judge me,
judge my whole book —
not a page.

because a page does not define me.

BLUSH

no more second guessing yourself.
no more hiding your true self.
you were meant to be seen.
you were meant to be heard.
you were meant to rule this beautiful world.

what is the colour of lonely?
it's neither too dark nor too bright.
it's the colour of us in muted hues.
it is afraid to stand out,
so it blends in with skin,
so easy to miss.
so hard to see.
such is the colour of lonely.

BLUSH

a flicker in the dark.
a memory from the past.
you come to me in pieces,
ripping me apart.

i thought i had left it all behind.
i thought i had buried everything inside.
but you were always one to creep up on me,
because monsters lurk only in the dark.

she was beautiful —
a mosaic of colourful, broken pieces,
letting the light within shine through,
and in turn, colouring everyone in her radiant hues.

i hope you are happy.
i hope you smile a lot.
i hope you still believe in love.
i hope you can still trust.
i hope the uncertainties of this world
haven't taken that away from you.
i hope you remember all the good times.
i hope you can forget everything bad.
i hope you are healing.
i hope you feel free.
i hope you understand this is just a journey,
not the end of the path.
i hope you still believe in magic.
i hope you still dream.
i hope you can see how special you are.
i hope you can feel how loved you are.
i hope your faith hasn't shaken,
because your journey towards yourself
has only just begun.

sometimes all i am doing
is seeking shelter
between the lines
of words that i write.

BLUSH

the pain will subside.
the tears will dry.
the cracks aren't permanent —
they are there just to let the light through.
the world hasn't collapsed.
the darkness isn't forever.
the sun still rises after it sets.
the flowers still bloom after they wither.
the memories will fade.
the scars will heal.
i promise it will get better.
just have faith.
just breathe.

i wish you never find out
the number of times
i almost reached out,
wanting to hear your voice —
wanting to know if you're doing okay
because I was not.

i hope you only see
this new version of me,
standing erect,
chin up, and looking ahead —
not the girl you once knew
with her heart on her sleeve.

i healed myself
by rearranging myself
until the pain faded away,
all my pieces glued together,
one by one,
with tenderness and love.

you tried to change me
from what i was
to what, in your eyes,
i could never be.
but here i am, different and happier.
because of you,
i am now brand new

BLUSH

darkness so magnetic
that it blinds
a soul so empty.
it devours your light,
an aura so dense
it makes you lose your way.
and when you try to fight your way out
it says,
stay another day!

— *depression*

sometimes i disappear within myself.
nobody even gets to know,
because i'm still here, smiling into the crowd.
it saves me the trouble of answering questions.
it's something i don't want to talk about.

sometimes i'm just a ghost,
suspended in empty space,
drifting between my thoughts,
trying to hold onto them,
but they just come and go.

it's not that i'm sad, or even in pain.
i'm just soul numb
and a little drained.
i just need some quiet
to feel like myself again.

it is in the fragility of life that we discover our true inner strength.

has it ever happened,
what you thought was a blessing
turned out to be a nightmare?

only to look back years later
and call it a blessing once again
because it made you the person you are today?

BLUSH

dark clouds in the gloomy brooding sky.
thunder and lightning at war with one another.
the howling winds mourning the loss of its lover.
the rain just pouring down,
drenching everything in its grief .

a bit like how i'm feeling from inside.

the hurtful things you once said
are finally starting to fade away.
your memories, barely a shadow,
and your voice,
an echo from far away.

BLUSH

somedays, there are so many thoughts
dancing inside of my head,
and i keep them all inside.
somedays, the voices in my head
keep screaming to be heard,
but i silence them with a smile.
somedays, my feelings
want to pour out of my heart and spill all over me,
but i lock them away so no one can see me
in colours of grief.

the days that i am most afraid

are also the days when

i am the bravest.

they say god works in mysterious ways.
i understand this now.
he took away everything i thought i needed,
leaving me empty and alone,
only to fill me with so much
that i felt my heart would explode.
i was too fragile to understand
this was needed to make me strong.
the decluttering only made space for more.
now i see things as i have never before —
unexpected love and simple joys
are all the blessings we need to survive.

do you hear your soul
calling out your name?
soft whispers,
soothing all the pain.

you thought i wouldn't survive.
you thought i would come running back.
but look at me now —
i glow from within,
even in the dark.

BLUSH

looking back and seeing
how far i've come
is the best view
there can ever be.

you are the sun,
not just a spark.
you are whole,
not just a half.
i hope you remember this
on days it gets dark.

BLUSH

i guess i ended up becoming a poem myself,
composed in the name of love.
sonnets of longing
tracing the curves of my body.
words like forever and eternity
gracing the lines.
i thought it was for love,
but it was just for the rhyme,
and like most love poems,
i was composed in the name of love
and forgotten in the name of love.

be that ray of sunlight
that knows it needs to shine,
and it forces the dark clouds to part
so that it can make its way through.

be that seed
who isn't scared of the darkness,
and grows strong enough
to tear the earth apart when it rises.

be that butterfly
who knows nothing but the safety of its cocoon,
but still has the courage to spread its wings
and fly like it always knew.

be the love
that always finds a way to spread warmth,
unaffected by harshness
the love that already exists within you and me.

BLUSH

everything becomes clear
when we close our eyes
and quiet our thoughts,
silence our voices
and calm our restless hearts.
everything makes sense
when we are still
and do the opposite of what
life has taught us to do,
which is to keep moving forward.

little battles won amidst big wars
are still victories worthy of celebrating.

BLUSH

talk to me.
confide in me.
tell me all your worries.
sink into me.
collapse into me.
my love will keep you warm.
let it all go.
crash land into me.
i am here to cushion your fall.

when your heart is full of love,
when your mind is at peace,
when your soul is in a state of gratitude,
when you are full of life,
write yourself a love letter
as you would do for a lover.
put words of love, hope,
faith, and encouragement
on paper.

tell yourself
how good you feel.
you didn't give up on yourself.
tell yourself
how strong you know you are
and how loved you will always be.
tell yourself
the good days will always come —
negativity is temporary and just a phase.
tell yourself
the joy the good times will bring with them
will be so fulfilling
that there will be no more space left
to brood over the bad times.
tell yourself
how proud you are to know someone like you.

write this love letter to yourself
and many such more.
read them to yourself
whenever you are feeling low
because, sometimes,
you just need to tell yourself
how happy you are to be you.

the path of healing is one
on which we must walk alone.
it is lonely and terrifying.
but it is the only way
we will come face to face
with our souls.
braving the shadows,
swimming through tears to get to the shore
and shedding layers that don't serve us anymore.

perhaps softness is all we need.

BLUSH

let's take a walk
along the curves of the words
i've written for you.
i want to show you
where you can seek refuge
when this world gets too much to bear.
where blankets of comfort,
coated in tender, loving words,
are waiting to engulf you.

When I started posting my poems on Instagram a few years ago, I didn't know what to write on my profile that would best describe my style of writing. So I just wrote – *Simple Words, Complex Feelings.* That is what Blush is: a collection of poems written in simple words about the complexities of love and life.

Thank you for taking out the time to read this book.

This book contains pieces of my heart and now they are yours to keep.

Mom and Dad
Thank you for everything that you do. I don't say it as often as I should, sometimes I don't say it at all, but I love you both, a lot. This book is for you. I hope I've made you proud.

Rahul
Thank you for always being there with your crazy ideas and unlimited supply of food. You are the best brother anyone could ask for.

My Dang and Jain family
Thank you for always being there.
Love you all.

Rachel and Freydis, this book would not exist without you guys. Your magic has brought an idea that was sitting in the shy corners of my mind to life.

Thank you for everything.

Shefali Dang is a Toronto based poet, she lives with her husband, two kids and a furry dog. She discovered her love for words and rhymes when she was in high school. That is when she realized that when the two came together, they could create beautiful stories and vivid imagery. Her lyrical verses effortlessly weave tales of love and life. Her poetry reflects the joys and challenges of nurturing relationships and cherishing everyday moments. She enjoys reading and immersing herself between the pages of a good book. Her creativity is not limited to poetry, she is also a self-taught photographer.

Instagram: @theshefalidang

www.ingramcontent.com/pod-product-compliance
Lightning Source LLC
Chambersburg PA
CBHW031103080526
44587CB00011B/809